INTERNAL WARS: RETHINKING PROBLEM AND RESPONSE

Max G. Manwaring

September 2001

FOREWORD

Dr. Max Manwaring wrote this monograph in response to the fact that today over half the countries in the global community are faced with one variation or another of asymmetric guerrilla war. Insurgencies, internal wars, and other small-scale contingencies (SSCs) are the most pervasive and likely type of conflict in the post-Cold War era. That the United States will become involved directly or indirectly in some of these conflicts is almost certain. The Balkans, Colombia, Mexico, Somalia, and the Philippines are only a few cases in point. Yet, little or no recognition and application of the strategic-level lessons of the Vietnam War and the hundreds of other smaller conflicts that have taken place over the past several years are evident.

The purpose of this monograph is not to find fault or identify villains. It is to draw from the lessons of the recent past to better prepare today's civilian and military leaders to meet the unconventional and asymmetric warfare challenges that face the United States and the rest of the international community. This country is in a new global security environment that involves the integration of free markets, technologies, and countries to a degree never before witnessed. The growling, nuclear-armed Soviet bear was relatively easy to understand and deal with. The many "smaller" threats—and benefits—that stem from global integration are not easy to understand and respond to. Yet, as the country that benefits most from global integration, the United States has a pressing national interest in maintaining and enhancing the new order. By coming to grips analytically with the most salient strategic lessons or rules that dominate contemporary SSCs, political and military leaders can maximize opportunities in the current and future chaos.

The Strategic Studies Institute is pleased to offer this monograph, the second of our "Studies in Asymmetry," as part of the ongoing refinement of our nation's understanding of the strategic risks and opportunities arising from asymmetry.

DOUGLAS C. LOVELACE, JR.
Director
Strategic Studies Institute

BIOGRAPHICAL SKETCH OF THE AUTHOR

MAX G. MANWARING is a Professor of Military Strategy at the U.S. Army War College. He is a retired U.S. Army colonel and Adjunct Professor of Political Science at Dickinson College. He has served in various civilian and military positions at the U.S. Army War College, the U.S. Southern Command, and the Defense Intelligence Agency. Dr. Manwaring holds a B.S. in Economics as well as a B.S., an M.A., and a Ph.D. in Political Science from the University of Illinois. A graduate of the U.S. Army War College, Dr. Manwaring's areas of expertise include theory of grand strategy, U.S. national security policy and strategy, military strategy, military and nonmilitary operations other than war, political-military affairs; and Latin America. Dr. Manwaring is the author and co-author of several articles, chapters, and reports dealing with political-military affairs. He is also the editor or co-editor of *El Salvador at War; Gray Area Phenomena: Confronting the New World Disorder; Managing Contemporary Conflict: Pillars of Success; Beyond Declaring Victory and Coming Home: The Challenges of Peace and Stability Operations;* and *Deterrence in the Twenty-First Century.*

SUMMARY

The end of the Cold War did not produce an end to internal or regional conflict and the expected peace dividend. Today, over half the countries in the international community are faced with one variation or another of asymmetric small (i.e., guerrilla) wars. Insurgencies, internal wars, and other small-scale contingencies (SSCs) are the most pervasive and likely type of conflict in the new world order. It is almost certain that, sooner or later, the United States will become involved, directly or indirectly, in many of these conflicts. It is also certain that the deplorable experience of Vietnam distorts and blurs American thinking about guerrilla insurgency. As a result, there appears to be little or no recognition and application of the strategic-level lessons of the Vietnam War and the hundreds of other smaller conflicts that have taken place over the past several years.

These lessons are not being lost on the new political actors emerging into the contemporary multi-polar global security arena. Ironically, strategies being developed to protect or further the interests of a number of new players on the international scene are inspired by the dual idea of evading and frustrating superior conventional military force within the global chaos. The better a power such as the United States becomes at the operational level of conventional war, the more a potential opponent turns to asymmetric solutions. Thus, the purpose of this monograph is to draw from the lessons of the recent past to better prepare today's civilian and military leaders for the unconventional and asymmetric warfare challenges that face the United States and the rest of the global community.

To help leaders come to grips analytically with the most salient strategic lessons and rules that dominate contemporary asymmetry, we do four things. First, we clarify the strategic lessons of Vietnam. These lessons provide a short list of fundamental rules for dealing with contemporary conflict. Second, with this as background, we develop lessons from several other guerrilla wars that have taken place since the end of World War II. The complementary lessons from 69 additional cases demonstrate important "intermediate" rules for playing in the contemporary global security arena. Third, we examine the future of guerrilla war. This examination includes an analysis of the signposts along the road to the 21st century and concludes that the hard-learned lessons of the past remain valid. Finally, we outline two "advanced" structural rules for generating strategic clarity and success in current and future conflict. All this, hopefully, will generate the broad strategic vision necessary to win a war—not just the battles, but the war itself.

The Fundamental Strategic Lessons of Vietnam: Relearning from the Theory and Experience of the Past.

If the lessons of Vietnam teach anything, they teach the need to go back to basics. The fact that the U.S. armed forces were never defeated on the Vietnam battlefield obscures another important fact of that war. Although American forces never lost a battle, in the end it was the Vietcong and their North Vietnamese allies who achieved their strategic objectives and emerged victorious. Americans thought they were fighting a limited war of attrition against a traditional enemy—dressed in black pajamas. The threat the South Vietnamese government and the United States had to deal with was not a limited or a traditional one. Rather, the Vietcong—on another level, and dressed in their comical black pajamas—were making unconventional preparations to take control of the state.

This reality takes us back to where we began. It takes us to the question: "How could the United States have won all the battles in Vietnam, but lose the war?" The answer is straight-forward. American leadership failed to apply the fundamental principles of military theory and grand strategy in that conflict. More specifically:

• The assessment of the nature of the conflict was incorrect.

• The strategic environment within which the war was taking place was misunderstood or ignored.

• The primary centers of gravity were not carefully or continually assessed, prioritized, or considered in nonmilitary (e.g., socio-political) terms.

• There was no appreciation of the centrality of rectitude and moral legitimacy in supporting the counter-guerrilla effort.

• These fundamental principles were not brought together and put into a strategic paradigm through which to understand and conduct the war.

The central unifying theme of these lessons is decisive. The instruments of national power must be organized, trained, and equipped within prescribed budgetary considerations. But, those actions must be preceded with clear, holistic, and logical policy direction—and the structure, roles, missions, and strategy that will ensure the achievement of the political ends established in that policy. This is a fundamental "rule" that is as valid for current and future conflict as it has been in the past.

Lessons from 69 Post-World War II Internal Wars: Intermediate "Rules" for Playing in the Contemporary Global Security Arena.

In the mid-1980s practitioners and academics deemed it important to begin to face the so-called Vietnam syndrome and try to understand the variables that make the difference between wining and losing asymmetric guerrilla wars. The intent was to improve prospects for success in contemporary and future internal conflict situations and to do a better job of protecting and advancing U.S. national interests in the developing global instability. One such effort, never widely publicized, was initiated in 1984 by then Vice Chief of Staff of the U.S. Army General Maxwell Thurman.

The results of most of the mandated research are available at the National Security Archives in Washington, DC. There is nothing really startling or radical about them. The results suggest basic security strategy and national and international asset management. Importantly, however, the research points out that no successful strategy, on either side of the conflict spectrum, has been formulated over the past 50 years that has not explicitly or implicitly taken into account *all* the following strategic dimensions—or wars within the general internal war. They are:

- A "legitimacy war" to attack or defend the moral right of an incumbent regime to exist.
- A more traditional police-military "shooting war" between belligerents.
- "Wars" to isolate belligerents from their internal and/or external support.
- A closely related "war to stay the course"—that is, the effort to provide consistent and long-term support to an ally.
- Intelligence and information "wars."
- "Wars" to unify multilateral, multidimensional, and multi-organizational elements into a single effective effort.

It is important to note that the application of these dynamic elements in a successful grand strategy subsumes a realistic strategic vision and policy that is based on the fundamental principles discussed in the previous section.

The Future of Asymmetric Internal Wars: Some Signposts on the Road Ahead.

Even though prudent armies must prepare for high risk low-probability conventional war, there is a high probability that the President and Congress of the United States will continue to require military participation in small internal guerrilla wars well into the future. These wars will likely have new names, new motives, and new levels of violence that will be a new part of the old problem. Nevertheless, whether they are called "Teapot wars," "Camouflaged wars," "Unrestricted wars," "Operations Other Than War," or something else, future guerrilla wars can be identified by the lowest common denominator of motive. And, as a corollary, whether they are considered "spiritual insurgencies," "commercial insurgencies," or anything else, guerrillas wars are the organized application of violent or nonmilitary coercion or threatened coercion intended to resist, oppose, change, or overthrow an existing government, and to bring about political change.

It is daunting and sometimes overwhelming to think of the implications for guerrillas, or other self-appointed saviors, who might employ nuclear, chemical, biological, electronic, and informational weapons to attain their objectives. Thus, although present and future asymmetric conflicts may have different trappings, it is imperative to remember the lessons of the past. The continuing relevance of relatively recent experience can be seen in ongoing conflicts. That is:

• Moral legitimacy remains the most important principle of the post-World War II era. It can been seen, as examples, in the Kurdish problem in Iraq, Iran, Turkey, and Russia from at least 1961 to the present; Sierra Leone since 1991; the Islamic Salvation Front in Algeria since 1992; and in Chechnya since 1999.

• Appropriate use of military force is still a key element in determining success or failure of counterguerrilla wars. Importantly, the irrelevance of heavy Russian military equipment and conventional training can be seen in the Peruvian effort against the Sendero Luminoso, and in the Ethiopian case.

• The logical need to isolate belligerents from sources of support is obvious in any number of contemporary cases. Two contemporary examples are Colombia and Chechnya. In Colombia, the insurgent alliance formed with narco-traffickers is providing generous financial assistance in return for protection of narcotics operations. In Chechnya—and earlier in Afghanistan—the war against Russian domination would be impossible without substantial outside aid from state and nonstate political actors.

• In this connection, the need to "stay the course" remains constant. Without outside aid and internal support, the Irish Republican Army could not function effectively in Northern Ireland. Likewise, the Middle Eastern Kurds would be unable to carry on their campaigns for national liberation.

• Intelligence and information are more vital than ever to the success or failure of contemporary guerrilla war. Some argue, for example, that the failure of the stability operations in Somalia was due in large part to a failure of the United States and United Nations (U.N.) to develop adequate and timely human intelligence. On the other hand, and as only one example, information campaigns have been key to the success of the Zapatista insurgency in Mexico.

• Unity of Effort is the last principle that will be noted here. Suffice it to say that the many problems of the U.N. operation in the Congo (UNOC), the U.N. operation in Somalia (UNOSOM II), the U.N. operations in the former Yugoslavia, and the NATO operations in Bosnia and Kosovo stem from a lack of unity of effort among the various players.

As in the past, to the extent that these factors or dimensions are strongly present in any given strategy, they favor success. To the extent that any one is absent, or only present in a weak form, the probability of success is minimal.

Two Advanced Structural "Rules" for Success in the Global Security Arena.

Two characteristics of asymmetric guerrilla threats have been identified as particularly significant. First, defense planners today cannot know precisely what sort of threats will emerge and what types will prove effective. Second, the effectiveness of asymmetric threats that have an impact will sooner or later decline as an enemy adjusts. Some argue that by maximizing conceptual and organizational adaptability and flexibility, the United States can assure that it will rapidly counter emerging asymmetric threats, and speed the process by which a threat becomes insignificant or ineffective. Phrased differently, in a time of strategic fluidity and asymmetry like the current one, the political actor that develops new concepts and concomitant leader judgment—and unifying organizational structure—better and more quickly than an opponent will have a decided advantage.

Given today's realities, failure to prepare adequately for small war (i.e., guerrilla) contingencies is unconscionable. At a minimum, there are two basic cultural and organizational imperatives. They are:

• Leader Judgment. In that context, there are several fundamental educational and cultural requirements to modify Cold War mind-sets and to develop the leader judgment that is needed to deal effectively with ambiguous, complex, politically dominated, multidimensional, multi-organizational, multinational, and multicultural internal war situations. The study of conventional war has always been considered to be essential preparation for leaders involved in war. The study of "unconventional" asymmetric war is no less essential.

• Unity of Effort. Operations at any level will achieve strategic clarity and maximum effectiveness as a result of integrating both horizontal and vertical planning and implementation processes from the outset. That is, integrating horizontal (i.e., multinational) political-military planning and operations with vertical national (e.g., U.S. interagency) political-military planning and operations achieves a synergy toward the achievement of an agreed political vision. These are two fundamental organizational mechanisms necessary to help eliminate "strategic ambiguity," "ad-hoc-ery," and "mission-creep."

Conclusions.

These are lessons that should have been learned from the U.S. experience in Vietnam, and the analysis of a large sample of other relatively recent small (i.e., guerrilla) wars. The value of the ideas or "rules" derived from this experience lies in their utility as a conceptual framework within which data from specific situations might be placed and understood. If American and other leaders consider these ideas not as a template, but, with serious intent, they may be able to translate battlefield courage, logistical superiority, and tactical victories into strategic successes in the current and future asymmetric global security arena.

INTERNAL WARS: RETHINKING PROBLEM AND RESPONSE

The end of the Cold War did not produce an end to internal or regional conflict and the expected peace dividend. Ethiopia, the Balkans, Sudan, Mexico, and the Philippines are cases in point. As this monograph is being written, over half the countries in the global community are faced with one variation or another on guerrilla war.[1] Insurgencies, internal wars, and other small-scale contingencies, then, appear to be the most pervasive and most likely type of conflict in the new world order. It is almost certain that, sooner or later, the United States will become involved in some of these small (i.e., guerrilla) wars. It is also certain that the deplorable experience of Vietnam distorts and blurs American thinking about guerrilla insurgency. Yet, the post-Vietnam experiences in aiding guerrillas in Afghanistan and helping to combat insurgents in El Salvador demonstrate that the United States can operate with or against guerrillas under diverse circumstances and achieve important objectives.[2]

What we hear and see in the year 2001 is not encouraging, however. Three examples should suffice to make the point. First, the debate regarding the transition of the armed forces into a viable instrument of U.S. national power for now and into the 21st century centers on a categorical need for X number of Army divisions, X number of Navy ships, and X number of Air Force squadrons. We also hear of the need to defend outer space and the need for a missile shield to protect the United States and its allies.[3] The questions unanswered in these debates are: "Why? For what purposes? Against whom? And, how will these forces be used to achieve a political end?" It would appear that the civilian and military leaders avoiding these questions are still expecting some equivalent of Soviet combined arms armies to come crashing into West Germany, or Iraqi armies to again maneuver in the open desert.

In this connection, there appears to be no recognition of the fact that the lessons of the Vietnam War, the Persian Gulf War, and any of the hundreds of smaller conflicts that have taken place over the past several years are not being lost on the new political actors emerging into the contemporary multipolar global security arena. Ironically, strategies being developed to protect or further the interests of a number of new players on the international scene are inspired by the dual idea of evading and frustrating superior conventional military force.[4] The better a power such as the United States becomes at the operational level of conventional war, the more a potential opponent turns to asymmetrical solutions.[5] Ralph Peters warns us that in current and future conflict, "Wise competitors . . . will seek to shift the playing field away from conventional military confrontations toward unconventional forms of assault . . . Only the foolish will fight fair."[6]

Third, U.S. policy tends to ignore the guerrilla threat in general instability and specific counterdrug efforts. Examples over the past several years from Thailand in Southeast Asia to Colombia in South America demonstrate that American advice, training, and equipment may be used only against illegal drug traffickers. That has been a deadly problem in a large number of lethal confrontations where it is virtually impossible to distinguish armed opponents as either insurgents or narcotraffickers—until after the fact, and probably too late. The rationale behind the practice of ignoring the guerrilla reality while confronting the illegal narcotrafficker threat within the same operational environment is that if the United States allows its advisors, weaponry, and equipment to be used against guerrillas, the country will slide down the slippery slope into another Vietnam. Thus, "We are committed to maintaining a line between counternarcotics and counterinsurgency."[7]

The primary implication here is that broad strategic concerns have played little part in the debates as to what to do with the billions of dollars allocated to national and global security. The United States has faced security problems on an ad hoc case by case and situation by situation basis. The American experience in Vietnam demonstrated that as far as logistics and operations were concerned, the United States succeeded in everything it set out to accomplish. At the height of the war, the Army was able to move almost a million soldiers a year in and out of Vietnam, feed them, cloth them, house them, supply them, and sustain them in the field. This was an operational-level task of enormous magnitude, and the U.S. logistical system was adequate to that task.[8] On the battlefield, the U.S. armed forces were unbeatable. In engagement after engagement—including the great Tet Offensive—the forces of the Viet Cong and the North Vietnamese Army were repeatedly defeated.[9] Yet, in the end, the military prowess of the United States did not prevail.

North Vietnam, not the United States, achieved its strategic objectives and emerged victorious. How could the United States have succeeded so well, but failed so miserably? The answers to those questions focus on the problem of ignoring fundamental strategic requirements and approaching strategic issues with operational solutions. That is the basis of this monograph. The purpose is not to find fault or identify villains. It is to draw from the lessons of the past to better prepare today's civilian and military leaders to meet the unconventional warfare challenges that will almost certainly face the United States and the rest of the global community in the future. As U.S. Army (Retired) Colonel Harry Summers expressed it, paraphrasing General Douglas MacArthur's guidance to the Army in 1935, the quintessential strategic lesson to be learned from the Vietnam War (or any other conflict) is to "bring to light those fundamental principles, and their combinations and applications, which, in the past, have been productive of success."[10]

Thus, we clarify the most salient lessons of Vietnam. These strategic-level lessons provide a short list of fundamental rules for dealing with contemporary conflict. Second, with this as background, we develop lessons from several other guerrilla wars that have taken place since the end of World War II. These complementary lessons from a large sample of 69 additional cases demonstrate important "intermediate" rules for playing in the contemporary global security arena. Third, we examine the future of guerrilla war. This examination includes an analysis of the signposts along the road to the 21st century and concludes that the hard-learned lessons of the past remain valid. Finally, we outline two "advanced" structural rules for generating strategic clarity and success in current and future conflict. By coming to grips analytically with the most important lessons or rules that dominate modern internal wars, political and military leaders should be able to develop the broad strategic vision necessary to maximize opportunities in the current and future global chaos and to win a small (i.e., guerrilla) war—not just the battles, but the war itself.

THE FUNDAMENTAL STRATEGIC LESSONS OF VIETNAM: RELEARNING FROM THE THEORY AND EXPERIENCE OF THE PAST

If the lessons of Vietnam teach anything, they teach the need to go back to basics. Sun Tzu prophetically argues that, "War is of vital importance to the State; the province of life or death; the road to survival or ruin. It is mandatory that it be thoroughly studied."[11] And Clausewitz reminds us that "The first, the supreme, the most far reaching act of judgment that the statesman and commander have to make is to establish . . . the kind of war on which they are embarking; neither mistaking it for, nor trying to turn it into, something that is alien to its nature."[12] Determining the nature of the conflict is thus "the first of all strategic questions and the most comprehensive."[13]

These dictums imply five highly interrelated and reinforcing strategic-level lessons that should have been learned from the American experience in Vietnam. They are the need to (1) carefully examine and define the nature of a given conflict; (2) fully understand the strategic environment within which the conflict is taking place; (3) determine the primary centers of gravity within that strategic environment that must be attacked and defended; (4) appreciate the "centrality of rectitude" in pursuing a given strategy or in supporting a given (e.g., counterinsurgency) effort; and (5) examine these lessons as a strategic whole. This last lesson takes us back to where we began and is the foundational basis for success.

Understanding the Nature of the Conflict.

The most fundamental principle that American leadership ignored in Vietnam was the need to understand the kind of conflict it was getting into. Then, as the war continued, civilian and military leaders tried to turn that guerrilla war into "something that it was not." As a consequence, the failure to correctly define the nature of the conflict provided an erroneous guiding basis to the subsequent conduct of the war. That, in turn, sealed the unsuccessful outcome of the war even as American troops began arriving in Vietnam. The final result was the exhaustion of the American army against a secondary guerrilla force, and the ultimate failure of the military to support the national policy of containment of communist expansion.[14]

In the tradition of the American way of war, civilian and military leaders thought that "kicking ass" and destroying the enemy military force was the goal of policy. Military violence was the principal tool.[15] At the same time, because a "limited war," such as that in Vietnam, implied a low-effort task unworthy of serious concern, it was something to be conducted with complaisance. It thus became a traditional war of attrition "writ small."[16] In that limited war of attrition, 58,000 Americans and 3.6 million Vietnamese died. In terms of total populations, 3.6 million

Vietnamese is proportionally equivalent to 27 million Americans.

Former Secretary of Defense Robert McNamara observed that "there are some people to whom life is not the same as to us, . . . we'd better understand that and write it down."[17] That is perhaps true, but in the strategic context of the Vietnam conflict, relative regard for life was not a simple cultural issue. General Vo Nguyen Giap explained unequivocally that the Vietnamese took those awful casualties because they were involved in a *national war of liberation*, and that the people participated enthusiastically in the resistance and consented "to make every sacrifice for its victory."[18]

Many American military officers and civilian officials complained that the war in Vietnam had been "won" militarily but "lost" politically—as if these dimensions of the conflict were not completely interdependent. In becoming involved in a modern guerrilla conflict—something relatively straight-forward such as that in Chechnya or something more complex such as the Colombian crisis—an actor is likely to be involved in a set of simultaneously waged political-psychological wars within a general conflict. In those terms, an actor will not be engaged only in a military war. Rather, as one of Clausewitz's translators, Michael Howard, points out—operational and technical military factors are in fact subordinate to the "forgotten" political-social-psychological dimensions of contemporary conflict. If the struggle is not conducted with skill and based on a realistic understanding of the situation in question, "no amount of operational expertise, logistical back-up, or technical know-how could possibly help."[19]

Thus, it is imperative that senior decisionmakers, policymakers, and their staffs correctly identify the nature of the conflict in which they are involved; determine the central strategic problem and the primary political objective associated with it; prioritize the others; and link policy, strategy, force structure and equipment, and coordinated political-economic-psychological-military campaign plans to solving the central strategic problem. This linkage encompasses Clausewitz's "forgotten dimensions of strategy" and what Sun Tzu indicates is the indirect approach to conflict.[20] The idea is that there are other—more effective—ways to "render the enemy powerless" than to attack his military force.[21] It follows that a political-psychological-military effort would be a potent combination of ways to control a conflict such as that experienced against the Vietcong guerrillas in Vietnam. Such a conceptual exercise may be difficult, but it is absolutely necessary given the obvious alternative.

Understanding the Strategic Environment.

Another reason for the American defeat in Vietnam was that U.S. leadership paid little or no attention to the strategic environment within which the conflict was taking place. Once the nature of the conflict has been defined, the next step in the counterinsurgency war process is the full consideration of the strategic situation—and the most important threats implicit in it. That is, the conceptual foundation from which to further develop a strategic vision for the successful pursuit of the war. The primary consequence of ignoring the strategic environment was complete frustration on the part of leadership and troops involved in the guerrilla war, and the American public at home.[22]

What happened was that American and South Vietnamese forces would conduct series after series of highly effective military operations that devastated the Vietcong infrastructure and continually forced them and their North Vietnamese allies to withdraw from the immediate battlefield. Yet, despite traditional defeat, the insurgents and their allies kept coming back. They kept coming back from different directions, and they were always refreshed, resupplied, and rededicated. Eventually, of course, they prevailed.[23]

Americans could not understand the tenacity and the persistence of the Vietcong guerrillas or *how* the enemy could keep coming back defeat after defeat. As a consequence, analysts argue that the U.S. leadership did not understand three crucial things. They didn't understand the enemy, they didn't really know their allies, and they ignored the geopolitical aspects of the general security environment.[24]

Understanding the Enemy. First, American leaders did not analyze the socio-political situation in Vietnam and did not understand the implications of the fact that the guerrilla war in which they were involved was only the latest in a long series of wars of national liberation against foreign invaders. Vietnamese guerrilla roots and mentality were located in struggles against the Chinese, against French colonialism, against the Japanese invaders during World War II, against the French again from the end of the Japanese occupation to the French defeat at Dien Bien Phu in 1954, and, finally, against American "neocolonialism." As a result, the North Vietnamese and their South Vietnamese guerrilla allies were involved in a total war for independence. The will to overcome the foreign invaders had been inculcated into generations of highly nationalistic patriots for well over 100 years.[25] General Giap summed up the socio-political situation in the following terms:

> The guiding principal of the people's war was long-term resistance and self-reliance. That inspired in the people and the army a completely revolutionary spirit which instilled into the whole people the will to overcome all difficulties, to endure all privations, the spirit of a long resistance, of resistance to the end.[26]

The Guerrilla Threat. Americans thought they were fighting a limited war of attrition against a traditional enemy—dressed in black pajamas. The threat the South Vietnamese government and the United States had to deal with was not a limited or a traditional one. Rather, the Vietcong—dressed in their comical black pajamas—were making unconventional preparations to take control of the state.[27]

At the strategic level, the Vietcong focused its primary—indirect—attack on the legitimacy of the corrupt and American-dominated South Vietnamese government. Aside from spectacular actions like the Tet Offensive and shows of force to keep South Vietnamese and American troops off-balance and frustrated, the main military effort was that of "armed propaganda." Operationally, the guerrillas expanded political, military, and support components and consolidated their position with the "masses." The purpose was to convince the people that the Vietcong was the real power in the country, and that the incumbent regime in Saigon was unwilling and unable to perform its fundamental security and service functions. Tactically, except for shows of force, the guerrillas operated in relatively small units with political, psychological, and military objectives—in that order. "Armed propaganda" was conducted not to "win," but to further discredit the South Vietnamese government and the Americans. It was also intended to give the country and the world the impression that the Vietcong was more powerful that it really was.[28]

Knowing Your Ally and the Associated Threat. Second, U.S. leadership did not take the trouble to get to know their allies. To be sure, some great friendships were generated between many American and South Vietnamese military and between some American and South Vietnamese civilians. Nevertheless, American civilian and military leadership did not understand that the struggle between Vietcong challengers and the incumbent South Vietnamese government was a struggle over the moral right to govern. American leaders did not fully appreciate the psychological-political fact that the Vietcong focus was not so much on soldiers and politicians as on social classes and groups. Guerrilla attacks on the South Vietnamese government were generally indirect and relied on societal grievances such as political and economic injustice, racial and religious discrimination, and debilitating internal corruption and unwelcome foreign domination.[29]

This is the essential nature of the threat from any insurgent organization, and it is here that any response must begin. A counterinsurgency effort that does not respond to legitimate internal socio-political concerns and deals only with enemy military capabilities is ultimately destined to fail. In Clausewitzian terms, the military instrument for success in war depends on the other two elements of the "remarkable trinity"—that is, military success depends on the perceived justice of the government's political objectives and the resultant popular passions.[30] The war in Vietnam is a case in point.

The Geo-strategic Environment and the Associated Threat. Third, the thread that allows an insurgency to develop, grow, and succeed is adequate freedom of action over time and space. Guerrillas maintain their freedom of action and movement through the establishment and maintenance of remote base areas, sanctuaries, and supply routes. At the same time, they establish and maintain supporting infrastructure within a population.[31] The Ho Chi Minh Trail provides a good example of how the United States failed to deal effectively with one geographical element in the strategic environment and one of North Vietnam's most effective geo-strategic weapons. The trail became a network of roads from North Vietnam through "neutral" Laos and Cambodia into South Vietnam. General Maxwell Taylor argues that, as early as 1961, he informed President Kennedy that the Vietcong insurgents could not be beaten as long as infiltration by means of the Ho Chi Minh Trail remained unchecked.[32] Tony Joes explains:

> The failure both to close the Trail and to adopt an alternative strategy that would have neutralized its effects also meant that Hanoi could fight on interior lines, a tremendous advantage. It meant that the enemy was free to invade South Vietnam continuously: The NVA's (North Vietnam Army's) colossal 1972 Easter (Tet) Offensive would have been quite impossible without the Laotian springboard. It meant that when hard

pressed by allied forces, the enemy could simply retreat into Laos or Cambodia. Thus the policies of the Johnson administration made a lasting, or even a temporary, American military victory impossible. And that fact, in turn, meant that attrition . . . would take longer than key segments of the American public would accept.[33]

Summary. The war in Vietnam was considered by American leadership to be a "unique" problem and dealt with on an ad hoc, piecemeal, and operational basis as each separate crisis or issue arose.[34] What was worse was that the assumptions upon which U.S.—and, thus, South Vietnamese—actions were based were not well-informed, were erroneous, or were ignored. As a consequence of not understanding the enemy, not knowing the entirety of the South Vietnamese situation, and not dealing effectively with the reality of the geo-strategic situation outside the boundaries of Vietnam—and not responding appropriately to the threats implicit within that strategic environment—the counter-guerrilla war could not be won.

Centers of Gravity and Implications for a Strategy of Success or Failure.

Another fundamental principle that U.S. leaders found too difficult to address was that of attacking centers of gravity.[35] Theoretically and practically, it is necessary to correctly determine and aggressively attack the primary sources of a political actor's physical, psychological, and moral strength. These are the hubs of "all power and movement on which everything depends."[36] And, as a result, centers of gravity provide the basic architecture from which to develop a viable ends, ways, and means strategy. Beyond attacking the traditional enemy military formations and some of their support structure, American leadership found that it was easier to deal with tactical and operational-level "nodes of vulnerability."[37] As a war of attrition dictates, an unconscionable number of people were killed and hurt, but the sources of Vietcong and North Vietnamese strength were virtually unscathed.

Michael Howard reminds us that an adequate response must be essentially a strategic political-economic-social-psychological-security effort. The most refined tactical doctrine, operational expertise, and logistical backup that are carried out by the optimum military or police structure in pursuit of a policy that ignores the strategic whole—to include the populace—will be irrelevant.[38] It must also be remembered that if one wants strategic clarity to optimize effectiveness, one must precede tactical and operational efforts with relevant policy direction—and an ends, ways, and means strategy to achieve it.

The major implication of this situation is that the primary centers of gravity defined in the guiding strategic vision constitute a possible set of simultaneously waged political-psychological-social-moral-military wars within a general conflict. In becoming involved in a war such as that in Vietnam, centers of gravity may change as the situation changes and the so-called wars-within-the-war will also change.[39] Strategy, of necessity, will also change. As an example, Clausewitz points of that:

> In countries subject to domestic strife [such as Vietnam], the center of gravity is generally the capital. In small countries that rely on large ones [such as the United States for South Vietnam and North Vietnam for the Vietcong], it is usually the army of their protector. Among alliances, it lies in the community of interest, and in popular uprisings, it is the personalities of the leaders and public opinion. It is against these that our energies should be directed . . . Not by taking things the easy way—using superior strength to filch [some piece of territory] preferring the security of this minor conquest to great success—but by constantly seeking out the center of his power, by daring to win all, will one really defeat the enemy.[40]

Summers provides some illustrations of the dynamism of the centers of gravity in the later part of the Vietnam conflict. After the Paris Accords of 1973, “one of the first questions [the North Vietnamese] asked was whether the center of gravity had shifted from the U.S-South Vietnamese alliance to new centers of gravity—the destruction of the South Vietnamese armed forces and the capture of Saigon."[41] Once the North Vietnamese determined that the alliance was indeed irrelevant, preparations were begun that led to the defeat in detail of the South Vietnamese army, the fall of Saigon, and the unconditional capitulation of the South Vietnamese government and the final unification of the country. Here the center of gravity changed three times—from the "community of interest" of the United States and South Vietnam, to the classical enemy military force, to the capital city.

A major implication here is the fact that centers of gravity must be attacked—and defended. It is as important for an attacker to take the necessary measures to defend his own centers of gravity as it is for him to deal with his opponent's centers of gravity. Again, and in this context, U.S. leadership failed to defend American public opinion against the full-scale "propaganda war" that was conducted by North Vietnam and its allies throughout the world. American leadership failed to understand that the "streets of Peoria" and the "halls of Congress" were decisive in determining the outcome of the war thousands of miles away in Vietnam.

It is important for senior leadership to remember that each facet of conflict has its corresponding threat and center of gravity. The basic problem is to reevaluate constantly the principal threat and the proper order of priority for the others. The secondary problem is to develop the capability to apply long-term political, moral, psychological, and economic resources—as well as military—against the various centers of gravity that a guerrilla or other type of war generates. Shrinking from these inevitable requirements for success in contemporary conflict only prolongs the struggle. Sun Tzu reminds us that, ". . . there has never been a protracted war from which a country has benefited."[42]

The Centrality of Rectitude and Moral Legitimacy.

A central principle that emerged out of the war in Vietnam was that of rectitude or moral legitimacy. The essential beginning of understanding the centrality of this principle in pursuing the counterguerrilla strategy against the Vietcong was to come to terms with the fact that the conflict was conducted in an essentially political-moral context. This umbrella concept focused on the moral right of the South Vietnamese government to govern and demonstrated that legitimacy constituted the central strategic problem. It was the hub of all power and movement on which virtually everything depended. Popular perceptions of right and wrong, poverty, lack of upward mobility, and corruption threatened the right—and the ability—of the South Vietnamese regime to conduct the business of the state. And, these popular perceptions were key to the outcome of the conflict.[43]

The primary objective of the Vietcong was to destroy and take control of the South Vietnamese government. By transforming the emphasis of the war from the level of military violence to the level of a struggle for moral legitimacy, the guerrillas could strive for total objectives—the overthrow of the government—instead of simply attempting to obtain leverage and influence for "limited" political, economic, or territorial objectives in the traditional sense. Thus, the use of indirect moral force permitted the Vietcong to engage in a secret and prolonged war—striking at the government's right to govern—while appearing to the people to pursue altruistic purposes. In these terms, this war was not an extension of politics. This war *was* politics. Thus, because it was a zero-sum game in which there would be only one winner, it was also a total war.[44]

The major implication here is that to counter this socio-political challenge, the government must first recognize what is happening and then be willing to acknowledge that its civil support is fragile and its control over the populace contested. General John R. Galvin argues that to establish its moral legitimacy, the government must address contentious, long ignored, but popular issues tied to key facets of national life—socio-political, economic, educational, juridical—as well as engaging the guerrillas on the battlefield.

> The resulting burden on the military institution is large. Not only must it subdue an armed adversary while attempting to provide security to the civilian population, it must also avoid inadvertently furthering the insurgents' cause. If, for example, the military's actions in killing 50 guerrillas cause 200 previously uncommitted citizens to join the insurgent cause, the use of force will have been counterproductive.[45]

Another set of implications is obvious. Every policy, every program, and every action taken by a government—and its external allies—involved in an internal war scenario must contribute positively and directly to developing, maintaining, and enhancing the ability and willingness of that regime to control its territory and govern its people in that territory with rectitude. This provides an umbrella of moral legitimacy and is the prime lesson for vulnerable governments in the coming decades.[46]

Indigenous and foreign allied leadership must realize that the highest priority must be to strengthen and legitimize the state. Thus, critical points about moral legitimacy must be understood at three different levels. First, regime legitimacy is the primary target of the insurgents. Second, the regime and its allies must protect and enhance moral legitimacy as the primary means by which that regime might survive. Third, a besieged government looking abroad for support against guerrillas—or to deny support to guerrillas—must understand that rectitude and legitimacy is a double-edged moral issue that will either assist or constrain foreign willingness and ability to become *effectively* involved.

Again, Sun Tzu reminds us that "Those who excel in war first cultivate their own humanity and justice and maintain their laws and institutions. By these means they make their governments invincible."[47]

Looking at the Strategic Whole.

The fact that the U.S. armed forces were never defeated on the Vietnam battlefield obscures another important fact of that war. American tactical and operational successes tend to dim the strategic defeat. Thus, there is a need to examine the problems and lessons of Vietnam as a strategic whole. This is the combination of fundamental principles which in the past have been the basis of success. In these terms, it is important to remember that success in any one component of grand strategy cannot generate overall success. Success only becomes a viable *possibility* when all the components of a strategy form a logical conceptual framework, architecture, or strategic paradigm within which judgments, comparisons, and data may be given meaning.

This reality takes us back to where we began. It takes us to the question: "How could the United States have won all the battles in Vietnam, but lose the war?" The answer is straightforward. American leadership failed to apply the fundamental principles of military theory and grand strategy in that conflict. More specifically:

• The assessment of the nature of the conflict was incorrect.

• The strategic environment within which the war was taking place was misunderstood or ignored.

• The primary centers of gravity were not carefully or continually assessed, prioritized, or considered in nonmilitary (e.g., socio-political) terms.

• There was no appreciation of the centrality of rectitude and moral legitimacy in supporting the counterguerrilla effort.

• These fundamental principles were not brought together and put into a strategic paradigm through which to understand and conduct the war.

The central unifying theme of these lessons is decisive. If a country such as the United States wants efficiency and effectiveness in a matter as crucial as war, the civil-military leadership must concern itself with two things. Clearly, the instruments of national power must be organized, trained, and equipped within prescribed budgetary considerations. But, those actions must be preceded with clear, holistic, and logical policy direction—and the structure, roles, missions, and strategy that will ensure the achievement of the political ends established in that policy. This fundamental "rule" is as valid for current and future conflict as it has been in the past.

LESSONS FROM 69 POST-WORLD WAR II INTERNAL WARS: "INTERMEDIATE" RULES FOR PLAYING IN THE CONTEMPORARY GLOBAL SECURITY ARENA

In the mid-1980s practitioners and academics deemed it important to begin to face the so-called Vietnam syndrome and try to understand the variables that make the difference between wining and losing guerrilla wars. The intent was to improve prospects for success in contemporary and future internal conflict situations and to do a better job of protecting and advancing U.S. national interests in the developing global instability. One such effort, never widely publicized, was initiated in 1984 by then-Vice Chief of Staff of the U.S. Army General Maxwell Thurman. He mandated the empirical examination of an initial sample of 43 (subsequently expanded to 69) internal wars that would (1) allow the testing of competing theoretical approaches (i.e., strategic paradigms) to internal guerrilla conflicts; (2) determine the extent to which the success or fail outcome of such conflicts is predictable; and (3) generate a new paradigm to improve prospects for success in future similar situations.[48]

The results of part of the mandated research were published in 1992.[49] There is nothing really startling or radical about them. The results suggest basic security strategy and national and international asset management. The theoretical construct of the SWORD model suggests that even though every conflict is situation specific, it is not completely unique. Throughout the universe, there are analytical commonalities at the strategic and high operational levels. Seven dimensions (i.e., dependent variables), each composed of multiple independent variables, determine the success or failure of an internal war. In essence, they may be considered "wars within the general war." In that connection, it should be emphasized that the resultant paradigm has power and virtue in part because of the symmetry of its application—both for a besieged government and its allies, and for a violent internal challenger and its allies. That is to say, no successful strategy—on either side of the conflict spectrum—has been formulated over the past 50 years that has not explicitly or implicitly taken into account *all* the following strategic dimensions—or wars within the general internal war.

They are (1) a legitimacy "war" to attack or defend the moral right of an incumbent regime to exist; (2) a more traditional police-military "shooting war" between belligerents: (3) "wars" to isolate belligerents from their internal and external support; (4) the closely related "war to stay the course"—that is, the effort to provide consistent and long-term support to a host government; (5) intelligence and information "wars"; and (6) "wars" to unify multidimensional, multilateral, and multiorganizational elements into a single effective effort. It is important to note that the application of these dynamic dimensions in a successful strategy subsumes that a realistic strategic vision and policy are based on the fundamental principles discussed in the "Strategic Lessons of Vietnam" section above.

The Legitimacy "War."

The data show that the moral right of a regime to govern is the most important single dimension in a counter-guerrilla war. Thus, a politically strong and morally legitimate government is vital to any winning internal war strategy. The rectitude and legitimacy of the incumbent regime is the primary target—the primary center of gravity—as far as the insurgent organization is concerned. In that connection, the interaction between an allied outside power and the incumbent government, especially with regard to the publicly perceived level of the "Americanization" of a conflict, is critical to success. A counterinsurgency campaign that fails to understand the lack of rectitude and morally legitimate governance problem and responds only to "enemy" military forces is very likely to fail.[50]

As an example, leaders on both sides recognized early in the conflict in El Salvador that this dimension would be key to success or failure for the insurgents or the government. Speaking for the insurgents, Guillermo M. Ungo identified the legitimacy of the regimes as the primary center of gravity in that situation.[51] President Jose Napoleon Duarte understood the problem and countered with a nationalistic program designed to preempt the efforts of the Forabund Marti National Liberation Front (FMLN) guerrillas. His argument was simple: "If the Christian Democrats demonstrate in El Salvador that a democratic system can bring about structured changes peacefully, then the polarized choice between domination by the rightist oligarchy and violent revolution by the Left will no longer be valid."[52]

The Shooting "War."

Experience affirms that military force should not be applied ad hoc in response to either political or military failure, or in an attempt to "try something that might work." If military force must be inserted into a nationalistic milieu, it should be done overwhelmingly at the outset. Nevertheless, the data indicate that the best possible use of "foreign" military personnel in an internal conflict is one variation or another on the "train the trainer" role. Accordingly, the "outside" forces that might be brought into most counterguerrilla situations do not necessarily need the skills required for success against combined arms armies on the north German plain. What they do need is a high degree of professionalism, the ability to insert themselves unobtrusively into a nationalistic environment, and to help build and equip an indigenous military force capable of achieving political and psychological as well as police-military objectives. In this regard, it is important for that security organization to have the mentality to engage guerrillas without alienating the citizenry.[53]

Successful examples of this type of effort would include U.S. Military Mobile Training Teams (MTTs) training the first *Cazador* (Hunter) units of the Venezuelan Army into superior organizations during 1961-64 and the Bolivian Ranger units that destroyed Che Guevara's guerrilla organization in Bolivia in 1968. This approach did not require many "foreign" troops; they were in relatively little physical danger; and they kept a low political profile.[54]

The "Wars" to Isolate the Guerrillas.

The objective here is for a belligerent to isolate his opponent politically, psychologically, and militarily from his primary sources of support and sanctuaries—whoever and wherever they may be. To ignore this dimension of internal conflict as too difficult and too dangerous in its domestic and foreign political-military ramifications is to deny the possibility of ultimate success.[55]

This dimension is clearly demonstrated in virtually all the 69 cases examined, but the classic example of this type of war is Greece, 1946-49. In this case, the Greek insurgent forces received logistical and other support from Greece's Communist neighbors—Albania, Bulgaria, and Yugoslavia.

This support included food, clothing, arms, ammunition, training, transit areas, replacement centers, field hospitals, and supply depots. Countermeasures undertaken to control those borders by the Greek government and the army failed to have any significant effect on reducing the offensive capabilities of the guerrillas. The Greek National Army was only capable of pushing its insurgent enemies from one area to another. In the north, the insurgents would simply move into adjacent Communist territory and subsequently reappear in another part of Greece. However, in the spring of 1949, the Yugoslavian and other frontiers were closed to the Communist guerrillas as a result of negotiations and political decisions made in London, Moscow, and Belgrade. Denial of the various external supporting facilities to the insurgents made it only a matter of a short time before the insurgency was brought under control.[56]

A more recent example of the isolation of belligerents from internal sources of support is found in the Italian "counterterrorism" case during the late 1970s and the early 1980s. The Red Brigades and the other 297 leftist groups claiming responsibility for various terrorist and insurgent acts were isolated from the rest of the Italian community as a result of the effects of the legitimacy war, the intelligence and information wars, and the paramilitary shooting war. As the "terrorists" withdrew more and more into their own compartmentalized secret organizational structure, isolation from the rest of the world became more and more complete. That separation from the outside world further restricted access to the internal Italian political reality, the capability to recruit new members, and the ability to organize significant actions.[57]

The "War" to Stay the Course.

All support to a besieged government or, conversely, to a supported violent internal guerrilla challenger, must be consistent to be effective. Examination of the post-World War II conflict spectrum clearly indicates that when military, economic, and/or political aid to a client was withdrawn by an "ally" or coalition of allies during a conflict, or when any of this support was provided inconsistently, the possibilities for success in the general war were minimal. The data indicate that when aid was provided consistently over the long-term, chances for success in an internal war were considerably enhanced. It must be remembered that an important center of gravity lies in the "community of interest" of the supporting ally(s) and the supported government or insurgent organization. In these terms, what happens politically and psychologically in capitals of the world thousands of miles from a "war zone" may be more decisive than any series of military engagements.[58]

A host of cases from the Algerian war, 1954-62; the Vietnamese reunification, 1954-73; the El Salvadoran war, 1980-89; the Afghan war, 1979-89, to the current situation in the former Yugoslavia provide examples of this phenomenon. Nevertheless, in most of the cases in which the British were involved, they managed to create the perception that they were "there to stay" until the conflict was clearly under control. This was the situation in Greece, 1946-49; Malaysia, 1948-60; and Oman, 1965-75, to mention a few. This was not the case in Aden, however. In 1966 Britain announced its intention to withdraw its security forces on the date when that country was to become independent in 1968. Importantly, this meant that the British would pull out of Aden regardless of the ability of the new government to deal with the ongoing insurgency. As a result, the intended government never really had a chance.[59]

The Intelligence and Information Wars.

Individual men and women lead, plan, execute, and support a given conflict. As a result, a major concern in an internal war must be individuals. The intelligence apparatus must be in place, or created, that can locate, isolate, and neutralize an opposing belligerent's organizational and leadership structure. The data demonstrate clearly that the best police, paramilitary, or military forces are of little consequence without appropriate and timely intelligence. Likewise, willing support to the state on the part of a majority of the populace, motivated by legal, democratic, and honest informational actions on the part of the government are directly related to the synergism and effectiveness of a counterguerrilla war. In the final analysis, legitimate long-term military and political power depend on the proverbial "hearts and minds" of a people.[60]

The key role of effective—or ineffective—intelligence is clearly demonstrated in the Cuban and Nicaraguan cases of 1956-59 and 1979, respectively. In these classic cases, the intelligence organizations of the Batista and Samoza regimes continued a "business as usual" attitude during the insurgencies. That is, priority targets tended to be the personal enemies and legitimate internal political opposition of the two dictators. Because of the misdirected effort and lack of concern for any kind of rectitude involving citizens—innocent or not—the real motives of the Cuban and Nicaraguan dictators came into focus. Consequently, the sacrifices necessary to press a fight against insurgents who promised serious reform were not readily forthcoming from either citizen or soldier—and the key element of moral legitimacy was totally subverted.[61]

A good example of an Information "War" against a violent internal enemy is, again, found in the Italian case. In that situation, the state and the media embarked on a strong countersubversive public diplomacy campaign. The objective was to expose and exploit the fact that the various left-wing, right-wing, and separatist, pacifist, and other subversive groups operating in Italy during the late 1970s and the early 1980s were not organizations of the masses. Rather, they were self-appointed elites whose goals were not what the people wanted or needed—those goals were what the insurgent leaderships wanted or needed. The antisubversive information "war" demonstrated that, for the Red Brigades and their allies, those Italians who were not fellow ideological "true believers" were not really people. As an example, the thousands of victims killed, maimed, or abducted by the would-be insurgents were not considered to be human beings deserving of some personal dignity. They were considered "tools of the system, pigs, and watch dogs." Moreover, the government and media exposed the fact that Red Brigadists considered everyone else—even other comrades on the Left—to be mere "shit." Their legitimacy was greatly eroded, supporters were obviously alienated, and counterinsurgent intelligence was willingly provided.[62]

The "War" for Unity of Effort.

This dimension of counterguerrilla war involves overcoming parochial bureaucratic interests, fighting "turf battles," overcoming cultural obstacles, and ensuring that all efforts are centered on the ultimate goal—success. That is to say, the necessary organization at the highest levels must exist to coordinate and implement an effective unity of political-diplomatic, socio-economic, psychological-moral, and security-stability efforts against those who would violently depose a government. Again, this applies equally to an organization that threatens an incumbent regime. In any case, the ability to accomplish these things in a manner acceptable to the populace is key. And, that equates back to legitimacy. Without an organization that can establish, enforce, and continually refine a holistic plan and generate consistent national and international support, authority is fragmented and ineffective in resolving the myriad problems endemic to survival in contemporary conflict—thus, failure.[63]

Ambassador Robert Komer has pointed out that unity of effort was a major deficiency in the Vietnam War.[64] This was also the case at the Bay of Pigs (Cuba) in 1961; Aden in 1968; and the Spanish experience in the Western Sahara in 1975-76. Others have observed that the "strategic ambiguity" of the past United Nations (U.N.) and current NATO efforts in the former Yugoslavia is also a result of a lack of national and international unity of effort. On the positive side of the unity of effort dimension, with the exception of the 1968 fiasco in Aden, British counterinsurgency experiences seem to dominate. For instance, an overall coordinator of all military and civil activities has usually been appointed by the prime minister. A committee of the cabinet provides periodic general direction and support of this individual. The coordinator has the authority to deal with people in his own government and with officials in the threatened country. Together, long-term and short-term mutually supportive objectives are determined and pursued.[65]

THE FUTURE OF GUERRILLA WAR: SOME SIGNPOSTS ON THE ROAD AHEAD

Even though prudent armies must prepare for high risk low-probability conventional war, there is a high probability that the President and Congress of the United States will continue to require military participation in small internal guerrilla wars well into the future.[66] The harsh realities of the new world disorder are caused by myriad destabilizers. The causes include increasing poverty, human starvation, widespread disease, and lack of political and socio-economic justice. The consequences are seen in such forms as social violence, criminal anarchy, refugee flows, illegal drug trafficking and organized crime, extreme nationalism, irredentism, religious fundamentalism, insurgency, ethnic cleansing, and environmental devastation.

The Problem.

These destabilizing conditions tend to be exploited by militant nationalists, militant reformers, militant religious fundamentalists, ideologues, civil and military bureaucrats, terrorists, insurgents, warlords, and rogue states working to achieve their own narrow purposes. As a result, the interdependent global community is experiencing "wars of national debilitation, a steady run of uncivil wars sundering fragile but functioning nation states and gnawing at the well-being of stable nations."[67] The threats to national and international stability will be gravely complicated by "1,000 other snakes with a cause"[68]—and the will to resort to illegal and asymmetric measures to achieve their nefarious objectives. In this security environment, military and police forces have little choice but to rethink security as it applies to guerrilla menaces that many governments have tended to wish away.

The Challenge.

Guerrilla wars will likely have new names, new motives, and new levels of violence that will be a new part of the old problem. Nevertheless, whether they are called "teapot wars,"[69] "camouflaged wars,"[70] "unrestricted wars,"[71] or something else, future guerrilla wars can be identified by the lowest common denominator motive. And, as a corollary, whether they are considered "spiritual" insurgencies, "commercial"[72] insurgencies, or anything else, guerrilla wars are the organized application of violent or nonmilitary coercion or threatened coercion intended to resist, oppose, or overthrow an existing government, and to bring about political change.[73] It is daunting, and sometimes overwhelming, to think of the implications for guerrillas, or other self-appointed saviors, who might employ nuclear, chemical, biological, electronic, and informational weapons to attain their objectives. The point remains, however, that whatever it is called, whatever rationale justifies it, whatever means it uses, guerrilla war is widely perceived as an effective means of achieving power and influence.

In this context, every guerrilla war will be unique. It will reflect the history, geography, and culture of the society in which it occurs. Yet, there will be analytical commonalities—and strategic-level principles—that continue to be relevant. Ian Beckett is eloquent when he states that "The past of guerrilla warfare and insurgency represents both the shadow of things that have been and of those that will be."[74]

The Reality.

Although present and future internal conflicts may have different trappings, it is important to remember the hard-learned lessons of the past. The continuing relevance of relatively recent experience can be seen in the basic elements that define threat and dictate response that are derived from the SWORD model, and that can been seen in ongoing conflicts.[75]

• Moral legitimacy remains the most important principle of the post-World War II era. It can be seen, as examples, in the Kurdish problem in Iraq, Iran, Turkey, and Russia from at least 1961 to the present; Sierra Leone since 1991; the Islamic Salvation Front in Algeria since 1992; and in Chechnya since 1999.

• Appropriate use of military force is still a key element in determining success or failure of counterguerrilla wars. Importantly, the irrelevance of heavy Russian military equipment and conventional training can been seen in the Peruvian effort against the *Sendero Luminoso*, and in the Ethiopian case.

• The logical need to isolate belligerents from sources of support is obvious in any number of contemporary cases. Two examples would include Colombia and Chechnya. In Colombia, the alliance formed with narcotraffickers is providing generous financial assistance in return for protection of narcotics operations. In Chechnya—and earlier in Afghanistan—the war against Russian domination would be impossible without substantial outside aid from state and nonstate political actors.

• In this connection, the need to "stay the course" remains constant. Without outside aid and internal support, the Irish Republican Army could not function effectively in Northern Ireland. Likewise, the Middle Eastern Kurds would be unable to carry on their wars for national liberation.

• Intelligence and information also remain vital to the success or failure of contemporary guerrilla war. Participants and observers argue, for example, that the failure of the stability operations in Somalia was due in large part to a failure of the United States and the U.N. to develop adequate and timely human intelligence about militia groups in that country. On the other hand, information campaigns have been key to the success of the *Zapatista* insurgency in Mexico.

• Unity of effort is the last principle that will be noted here. Suffice it to say that the many problems of the U.N. operation in the Congo (UNOC), the U.N. operation in Somalia (UNOSOM II), the U.N. operations in the former Yugoslavia, and the NATO operation in Kosovo stem from a lack of unity of effort among the various military contingents making up the specific force.

The Task.

Steve Metz and others have identified two characteristics of asymmetric guerrilla threats that are particularly important. First, defense planners today cannot know precisely what sort of threats will emerge and what types will prove effective. Second, the effectiveness of asymmetric threats that have an impact will sooner or later decline as an enemy adjusts. Metz argues that by maximizing conceptual and organizational adaptability and flexibility, the United States can assure that it will rapidly counter emerging asymmetric threats, and speed the process by which a guerrilla threat becomes insignificant or ineffective. Phrased differently, in a time of strategic fluidity and asymmetry like the current one, the political actor that develops new concepts and concomitant leader judgment—and unifying organizational structure—better and more quickly than its opponents, will have a decided advantage.[76]

Conclusions.

Victory in any kind of war—including internal guerrilla war—is not simply the sum of the battles won over the course of a conflict. Rather, it is the product of connecting and weighting the various elements of national power within the context of strategic appraisals, strategic vision, and strategic objectives. Sun Tzu warns us that "in war, numbers alone confer no advantage. Do not advance relying on sheer military power."[77] The promulgation of such a concept requires a somewhat different approach to modern conflict than that generally used by the United States over the past several years.

The strategic paradigm outlined above acknowledges the fact that the ultimate outcome of any counterinsurgency effort is not primarily determined by the skillful manipulation of violence in the many military battles that take place once a war of this nature is recognized to have begun. Rather, control of the situation is determined by the level of moral legitimacy; organization for unity of effort; type and consistency of support, intelligence and information; the ability to reduce internal and external aid to the insurgents; and the discipline and capabilities of the security organization involved in the "shooting war." To the extent that these factors are strongly present in any given strategy, they favor success. To the extent that any one component of the model is absent, or only present in a weak form, the probability of success is minimal.

TWO "ADVANCED" STRUCTURAL RULES FOR SUCCESS IN THE GLOBAL SECURITY ARENA

The United States is embroiled in a world of dangerous uncertainty in which time-honored concepts of national security and the classical military means to attain it, while still necessary, are no longer sufficient. In becoming involved in modern conflict—relatively straightforward guerrilla war as in Chechnya or something more complex such as the Colombian crisis—a player is likely to be involved in a set of simultaneously waged political-psychological wars within a general conflict. In this world, in which one or a dozen political actors are exerting differing types and levels of power within a set of cross-cutting alliances, the playing field, rules, and players are more complex, and identifying the objectives of the game is more perplexing.

The political-military complexity of contemporary conflict requires the highest level of strategic thought and exceptional civil-military and military-military diplomacy, cooperation, and coordination. This issue dominates insurgency and other internal wars at two levels—the need to understand the nature of unconventional conflict, and the high levels of cooperation needed to deal with it. The first requirement pertains to the development of leader judgment. The second imperative involves the organization for unity of effort. Substantive changes in both the leadership development and unity of effort areas of concern require a carefully staffed, phased, and long-term validation, planning, and implementation program. The recommended basic direction for such efforts is outlined below.

Leader Judgment.

The study of the fundamental nature of conflict has always been the philosophical cornerstone for understanding conventional war. It is no less relevant to nontraditional war. In the past, some wars—such as that in Vietnam—tended to be unrealistically viewed as providing military solutions to military problems. Presently, the complex realities of these kinds of wars must be understood as a holistic process that relies on various civilian and military agencies and contingents working together in an integrated fashion to achieve common political ends.[78]

Given today's realities, failure to prepare adequately for small war (i.e., guerrilla) contingencies in unconscionable. At a minimum, there are eight basic educational and cultural imperatives to modify Cold War mind-sets and to develop the leader judgment needed to deal effectively with complex, politically dominated, multidimensional, multiorganizational, multinational, and multicultural internal war situations. They are:

• Concepts from "asymmetry," "center of gravity," "deterrence," and "enemy" to "victory" and "war" must be reconsidered and redefined for intrastate conflict.

• Civilian and military leaders at all levels must learn the fundamental nature of subversion and insurgency with particular reference to the way in which force can be employed to achieve political ends and the way in which political considerations affect the use of force. In addition, leaders need to understand the strategic and political-psychological implications of operational and tactical actions.

• Civilian and military leaders at all levels must learn that power is not simply combat firepower directed at an enemy military formation or industrial capacity. Power is multilevel and combined "hard" and "soft" political, psychological, moral, informational, economic, societal, military, police, and civil bureaucratic activity that can be brought to bear directly and indirectly within a given security environment.

• Civilian and military personnel are expected to be able to operate effectively and collegially in coalitions or multinational contingents. They must also acquire the ability to deal collegially with civilian populations, and local and global media. As a consequence, efforts that enhance interagency as well as international cultural awareness, such as civilian and military exchange programs, language training programs, and combined (multinational) exercises must be revitalized and expanded.

• In that connection, planners and negotiators who will operate at the strategic and high operational levels must be nurtured to function in coalitional decisionmaking and planning situations that can blend U.S. deliberate planning processes with concurrent multinational and multiorganizational practices. Additionally, there is a critical requirement to teach people how to put a campaign plan together using a combination of civil and military resources to achieve a single comprehensive political aim.

• Leaders must learn that an intelligence capability several steps beyond the usual is required for small internal wars. This capability involves active utilization of intelligence operations as a dominant element of both strategy and tactics. Thus, commanders at all levels must be responsible for collecting and exploiting timely intelligence. The lowest echelon where adequate intelligence assets have been generally concentrated is the division or brigade. Yet, operations in small wars such as insurgencies are normally conducted independently by battalion and smaller units.

• Civilian and military leaders must learn the totality of guerrilla wars. These small, intrastate wars are not a kind of appendage—a lesser or limited thing—to the more comfortable conventional military paradigm. They are a great deal more.

• Negotiations, agreements, and accords notwithstanding, guerrilla war is a zero-sum game in which there is only one winner.

• Finally, leader development must prepare military peacekeepers (i.e., peace enforcers) to be effective war fighters. Political actors in an intrastate conflict are likely to have at their disposal an awesome array of conventional and unconventional weaponry. The "savage wars of peace" have and will continue to put military forces and civilian support contingents into harm's way.

Unity of Effort.

Continuous and cooperative planning among and between national and international civilian and military organizations, beginning with a strategic assessment of the situation, can establish a mechanism for developing a common vision for ultimate political success (i.e., strategic clarity). Then, shared goals and objectives, a broad understanding of what must be done or not done or changed, and a common understanding of possibilities and constraints will generate an overarching political military campaign plan that becomes the basis for developing subordinate plans that will make direct contributions to the achievement of the desired political goals and objectives. Thus, the roles and missions of the various civilian and military elements evolve deliberately—rather than in response to "mission creep"—as the situation changes to accommodate progress toward the achievement of a mutually agreed political vision.[79]

In these terms, operations will achieve strategic clarity and maximum effectiveness as a result of integrating both horizontal and vertical planning and implementation processes from the outset. That is, integrating horizontal (i.e., multinational) political-military planning and operations with vertical national (e.g., U.S. interagency) political-military planning and operations achieves a synergy toward the achievement of an agreed political vision. Two fundamental organizational mechanisms are necessary to help eliminate "ad-hoc-ery" and to help ensure vertical and horizontal unity of effort. They are:

• A national executive-level management structure that can and will ensure continuous cooperative planning and execution of policy among and between the relevant U.S. civilian and military agencies (i.e., vertical coordination). That organizational structure must also ensure that all civil-military action at the operational and tactical levels directly contributes to the achievement of an agreed U.S. national strategic political vision.

• An *ad hoc* international executive-level management structure that can—when necessary—integrate coalition military, international organization, and nongovernmental organization processes with American political-military planning and implementing processes (i.e., horizontal coordination). That organization, too, must ensure that all multilateral civil-military actions directly contribute to the internationally agreed political vision.

Summary and Conclusions.

In sum, the lessons from over a half-century of bitter experience suffered by governments involved in dealing with guerrilla wars, and similar global destabilizers, show that a given international intervention often ends short of achieving the desired peace. Too often this is because short-, mid-, and long-term objectives are irrelevant or unclear, the "end-game" is undefined, consistent and appropriate support is not provided, and national and international civil-military unity of purpose remains unachieved. Thus, despite acknowledged difficulties, it is imperative to develop leaders and organizational structures that can generate strategic clarity and make it work.

Even though every conflict situation differs in time, place, and circumstance, none is ever truly unique. Throughout the universe of contemporary guerrilla war, there are salient analytical commonalities. The final outcome of conflicts such as those in Vietnam or Colombia—or the nearly 100 conflicts the U.N. Security Council has recognized since 1990 as destabilizing intrastate struggles—is not determined primarily by the skillful manipulation of violence on the battlefield. Control of the situation and its resolution are determined by the qualitative leader judgments and the synergistic organizational processes established before, during, and after a small internal war is politically recognized to have begun. These are the fundamental components of strategic clarity. And strategic clarity is essential to success in the new millennium.

AFTERWORD

These are the lessons that should have been learned from experience in 69 relatively recent small (i.e., guerrilla) wars. The value of the ideas or rules derived from this experience lies in their utility as a conceptual framework within which data from specific situations might be placed and understood. If U.S. and other leaders consider these ideas not as a template, but with serious intent, they may be able to translate battlefield courage, logistical superiority, and tactical victories into strategic successes in the current and future global security arena.

ENDNOTES

1. Guerrilla war is defined as a small war. The word comes from the Peninsular Campaign in Spain during the Napoleonic Wars. The data in this note can be found in *World Conflict & Human Rights Map 2000*, prepared by PIOOM for IIMCR with the support of the Goals for Americans Foundation, St. Louis, MO.

2. This is an argument developed in Anthony James Joes, *America and Guerrilla Warfare*, Lexington, KY: The University Press of Kentucky, 2000, pp. 2-4.

3. For succinct reviews of these issues, see: "Rumsfeld's defense dilemma," *The Economist*, June 30-July 6, 2001, pp. 25-26; and "Missile defenses: What's the real point?" *The Economist*, July 21-27, 2001, p. 9.

4. As one important example, see: Qiao Liang and Wang Xiangsui, *Unrestricted Warfare*, Beijing: PLA Literature and Arts Publishing House, 1999.

5. Steven Metz and Douglas V. Johnson II, *Asymmetry and U.S. Military Strategy: Definition, Background, and Strategic Concepts*, Carlisle Barracks, PA: Strategic Studies Institute, 2001.

6. Ralph Peters, "Constant Conflict," *Parameters*, Summer 1997, p. 10. See also "The Culture of Future Conflict," *Parameters*, Winter 1995-96, pp. 18-27.

7. This and subsequent assertions are derived from statistical tests based on interviews with more than 400 civilian and military officials and scholars with direct experience in 69 internal conflicts. The effort

was originally mandated by Vice Chief of Staff of the U.S. Army General Maxwell Thurman during 1984-86. It was subsequently taken up by Commander-in-Chief, U.S. Southern Command General John R. Galvin; Commander-in-Chief, U.S. Southern Command General Fred F. Woerner, Jr.; and others during from 1986-95. The model predicts at an impressive 88.37 percent of the cases examined, and is statistically significant at the .001 level. The model, originally called SSI 1 and SSI 21, has also been called the SWORD model. The *SWORD Papers*, although long out of print, are archived in their entirety by a private research organization, the National Security Archives, in Washington, DC. The quote, however, is taken from a formal statement made by U.S. Department of State Director of Andean Affairs Phil Chicola at the conference on "Landpower and Ambiguous Warfare: The Challenge of Colombia in the 21st Century," Carlisle, PA, U.S. Army War College, December 10-11, 1998. Mr. Chicola reaffirmed that position again in a conversation with the author on February 2, 2001, in Miami, FL. Hereinafter cited as "Author interviews."

8. Several diverse sources agree on these and subsequent assertions. They include, *inter alia*: Eric M. Bergerud, *The Dynamics of Defeat: The Viet Nam War in Hau Nghia Province*, Boulder, CO: Westview Press, 1991; Phillip B. Davidson, *Viet Nam at War: The History, 1946-1975,* Norton, OK: Providio Press, 1988; Bernard B. Fall, "Indochina, 1946-1954" and "South Viet-Nam, 1956 to November 1963," in D.M. Condit, and others, eds., *Challenge and Response in Internal Conflict: The Experience in Asia,* Volume I, Washington, DC: The American University Center for Research in Social Systems, 1968, pp. 237-266, 333-368; Michael A. Hennessy, *Strategy in Viet Nam: The Marines and Revolutionary Warfare in I Corps, 1965-1972*, Westport, CT: Praeger, 1997; Richard A. Hunt, *Pacification: The American Struggle for Viet Nam's Hearts and Minds*, Boulder, CO: Westview Press, 1995; Andrew F. Krepinevich, Jr., *The Army and Viet Nam*, Baltimore, MD: Johns Hopkins University Press, 1986; Bruce Palmer, Jr., *The Twenty-Five-year War: America's Military Role in Vietnam*, Lexington, KY: The University Press of Kentucky, 1984; Dave Richard Palmer, *Summons of the Trumpet*, San Rafael, CA: Presidio Press, 1978; Jeffrey Race, *War Comes to Long An*, Berkeley: University of California Press, 1972; U.S. Grant Sharp, *Strategy for Defeat: Viet Nam in Retrospect*, San Rafael, CA: Presidio Press, 1978; and Harry G. Summers, Jr., *On Strategy*, Carlisle Barracks, PA: Strategic Studies Institute, 1989, Fifth Printing. Hereinafter cited as *Bergerud, et.al.*

9. *Ibid.*

10. Summers, p. 121.

11. Sun Tzu, *The Art of War*, Samuel B. Griffith, trans., London: Oxford University Press, 1971, p. 63.

12. Carl von Clausewitz, *On War*, Michael Howard and Peter Paret, ed. and trans., Princeton, NJ: Princeton University Press, 1976, p. 88.

13. *Ibid.*, pp. 88-89.

14. Summers, p. 1.

15. Author interviews; and *Bergerud*, et.al.

16. Author interviews.

17. Quote attributed to former Secretary of Defense Robert McNamara in David K. Shipler, "Robert McNamara Meets the Enemy," *New York Times Magazine*, August 10, 1997, p. 50.

18. General Vo Nguyen Giap, *People's War, Peoples' Army*, New York: Frederick A. Praeger, 1962, p. 34.

19. Michael Howard, "The Forgotten Dimensions of Strategy" in *The Causes of War*, London: Temple-Smith, 1981, pp. 101-115.

20. Sun Tzu, pp. 63-64, 77-79.

21. Clausewitz, pp. 92-93.

22. Bergerud, *et.al.*; and Author interviews.

23. *Ibid.*

24. *Ibid.*

25. *Ibid.*

26. Giap, p. 36.

27. Author interviews.

28. *Ibid.*; Jeffrey Race, *War Comes to Long An: Revolutionary Conflict in a Vietnamese Province,* Berkeley, CA: University of California Press, 1972; Edward G. Lansdale, *In the Midst of Wars: An American's Mission to Southeast Asia,* New York: Harper and Row, 1972; John J. McCuen, *The Art of Counter-Revolutionary War: The Strategy of Counterinsurgency,* Harrisburg, PA: Stackpole Books, 1966; Robert W. Komer, *Bureaucracy Does Its Thing: Institutional*

Constraints on US- GVN Performance in Vietnam, Santa Monica, CA: Rand Corporation, 1972.

29. *Ibid.*

30. Clausewitz, pp. 80-81; 89.

31. Author interviews.

32. Maxwell D. Taylor, *Swords and Plowshares*, New York: Norton, 1972, p. 247; Norman B. Hannah, *The Key to Failure: Laos and the Viet Nam War*, Lanham, MD: Madison Books, 1987.

33. Joes, pp. 241-242.

34. Author interviews; Summers, p. 1.

35. Author interviews

36. Clausewitz, p. 596.

37. Author interviews.

38. Howard.

39. Clausewitz.

40. *Ibid.*

41. Summers, p. 83.

42. Sun Tzu, p. 73.

43. Author interviews.

44. *Ibid.*

45. General John R. Galvin, "Uncomfortable Wars: Toward a New Paradigm," *Parameters,* December 1986, pp. 2-8.

46. Author interviews.

47. Sun Tzu, p. 88.

48. This research is based on more than 400 interviews conducted by Dr. Max G. Manwaring and Colonel Alfred W. Baker, noted above in endnote 7. Additionally, it should be understood that the SWORD model

is statistically significant at the .001 level, and the adjusted R square equals .900. That is to say that the SWORD model predicts at about 90 percent. Six models were tested: the SWORD model, two U.S. Southern Command models proposed by General Paul Gorman at different times, a Central Intelligence Agency model, and General Sir Robert Thompson's model. General Gorman's second model tested closest to the SWORD model at R square equals .727. Other models with similar variables include those of General Vo Nguyen Giap ("Factors of Success"), John Norton Moore ("Radical Regime Syndrome"), Barry M. Blechman ("Force without War"), and Bard E. O'Neill ("Insurgency in the Modern World").

49. The first publication of the paradigm dealt specifically with 43 very closely defined "insurgencies," in Max G. Manwaring and John T. Fishel, "Insurgency and Counterinsurgency: Towards a New Analytical Approach," *Small Wars & Insurgencies*, Winter 1992, pp. 272-305. That work and the original SWORD effort have been validated in Edwin G. Corr and Stephen Sloan, eds., *Low-intensity Conflict: Old Threats in a New World*, Boulder, CO: Westview Press, 1992; and John T. Fishel, ed., *The Savage Wars of Peace: Toward a New Paradigm of Peace Operations*, Boulder, CO: Westview Press, 1998. Finally, the SWORD model has generated and informed a slowly growing literature dealing with contemporary conflict that has been reviewed by Ernest Evans, "Our Savage Wars of Peace," *World Affairs*, Fall 2000, pp. 90-94. Hereafter cited as *SWORD Papers*.

50. *Ibid.*

51. Guillermo M. Ungo, "The People's Struggle," *Foreign Policy*, Fall 1983, pp. 51-63; and Author interviews.

52. Jose Napoleon Duarte, *Duarte: My Story*, New York: G. P. Putman's Sons, 1986, p. 279; and Author interviews.

53. *SWORD Papers*.

54. *Ibid.*

55. *Ibid.*

56. *Ibid.*

57. This and the subsequent statement regarding the Italian case are consensus statements based on author interviews with senior Italian Caribineiri officials. The author is particularly indebted to General Carlo Alfiero for his guiding remarks. However, the intent is to

allow anonymity for those who object to their names being made public. Thus, these statements are cited as author interviews.

58. *SWORD Papers.*

59. *Ibid.*

60. *Ibid.*

61. *Ibid.*

62. Author interviews.

63. *SWORD Papers.*

64. Komer.

65. *SWORD Papers.*

66. The reality of this assertion is demonstrated in former-President Clinton's speech that opened the summit meeting of world leaders at the U.N. in September 2000. In that speech, he urged the gathering to prepare national and international institutions for a new age in which unilateral and international forces will have to "reach rapidly and regularly inside national boundaries to protect threatened people." *New York Times*, September 7, 2000, p. 1.

67. Leslie H. Gelb, "Quelling the Teacup Wars," *Foreign Affairs*, November-December 1994, p. 5.

68. Author interviews.

69. Gelb.

70. B. H. Liddlle-Hart, *Strategy*, second revised edition, New York: Signet, 1967, p. 367.

71. Qiao, pp. 10-11.

72. Steven Metz, *The Future of Insurgency*, Carlisle Barracks, PA: Strategic Studies Institute, 1993.

73. Field Manual 90-8, *Counterguerrilla Operations*, Washington, DC: Headquarters, Department of the Army, 1986.

74. Ian Beckett, "Forward to the Past: Insurgency in Our Midst," *Harvard International Review*, Summer 2001, p. 63.

75. The assertions in this section are derived from author interviews.

76. Metz, p. 15.

77. Sun Tzu, p. 122.

78. Author interviews with Lieutenant General William G. Carter III, U.S. Army (Retired) on November 30, 1998, and March 2, 1999, in Washington, DC. Also, an important contribution to this issue has been made by United Kingdom General Frank Kitson, *Warfare as a Whole*, London: Faber and Faber, 1987.

79. Author interview with General John R. Galvin, U.S. Army (Retired) on August 6, 1997, in Boston, MA. The complete interview is included in the Spring 1998 special issue of *Small Wars & Insurgencies*, Vol. 9, No. 1.

Author
Dr. Max G. Manwaring

www.ingramcontent.com/pod-product-compliance
Ingram Content Group UK Ltd.
Pitfield, Milton Keynes, MK11 3LW, UK
UKHW041838200726
13854UKWH00003BA/1199

9 781312 376519